prayer
spa

prayer is intimacy with God
and contemplation of the invisible

—saint gregory of nyssa

prayer
spa

ancient treatments for the modern soul

jennifer anna rich

paraclete press brewster, massachusetts

2019 First Printing
Prayer Spa: Ancient Treatments for the Modern Soul
Copyright © 2019 Jennifer Anna Rich
ISBN 978-1-64060-182-6

Library of Congress Cataloging-in-Publication Data
Names: Rich, Jennifer Anna, 1962- author.
Title: Prayer spa : ancient treatments for the modern soul / Jennifer Anna
  Rich.
Description: Brewster, MA : Paraclete Press, Inc., 2019.
Identifiers: LCCN 2018045605 | ISBN 9781640601826 (trade paper)
Subjects: LCSH: Prayer–Christianity.
Classification: LCC BV215 .R53 2019 | DDC 248.3/2–dc23
LC record available at https://lccn.loc.gov/2018045605

10 9 8 7 6 5 4 3 2 1

Published by Paraclete Press
Brewster, Massachusetts
www.paracletepress.com

Printed in the United States of America

contents

introduction

"true inner prayer is to stop talking
and to listen to the wordless voice of God
within our heart."

—metropolitan kallistos of diokleia

do you yearn for the beauty of prayer each morning?
do you believe that God made you to desire intimacy with Him?
do you wish to offer care to your own soul?

prayer spa is an invitation to the modern person
to nourish their mind, body, and soul
through contemplative prayer.

the wisdom of the prayer spa is nothing new.
these prayers are essential
a gift from the early church
largely forgotten in this modern world.

mind . . . expand your mind
with intention, attentiveness, and memorized prayer.

body . . . supple your body
through movement, stretching, and embodied prayer.

soul . . . nourish your soul
by dwelling with God in stillness and focused prayer.

breathe deeply of this prayerful way of holiness
this gentle instruction for each day's offering.

encounter the presence of God as an interior experience
as you allow Christ to pierce your heart with pure love
in ever-deepening layers of prayer.

one

mind . . . body . . . soul

expand your mind, supple your body, nourish your soul

"the christian is like someone who lives in
three dimensions in a world in which
the majority of people live in two."

—metropolitan anthony bloom

you are a gifted creature
created in the image of God

given the gifts of mind . . . body . . . soul.

dip your toe into living water and drench your soul in prayer.

how can i begin?
you ask.

begin with intention.
begin with practice.
begin with love.

therapy.

humbly, we approach the divine
daily.

at first it feels like hard work
then it becomes familiar
soon we don't feel whole without it.

the key is
regardless of feelings or emotions
you just show up

at the appointed time
for this conscious engagement with God
for this daily therapy . . . prayer.

drench.

while secular society holds in high esteem
the mind and the body

the soul dwells in mystery
and has been forgotten by the quickening world.

but for those of us who remember
the three created elements of our personhood
we yearn to enter into communion with our Creator
to drench our whole selves
mind, body, and soul
in prayer.

mind.

train your mind to pierce
through the roar of voices
undistracted, to a single focus.

this recalls the stillness of the desert
where our monastic fathers and mothers
honed their communion with a personal God.

science agrees with prayer
offering evidence of its healing powers
and the positive change it effects in the human brain.

sculpt your mind daily with active love
to increase trust and decrease worry
to dwell in the Kingdom of God.

massage your attention span
to align and extend its reach.

memorize prayers, scriptures, and psalms
to lift mind and soul
wrap them together in white cloth.

body.

expand your daily prayer life
to include movement

prostrating, bowing, stretching, lifting hands
these express our humility, adoration, gratitude, and praise
with our whole bodies before God.

together, these movements can become a liturgical dance
integrated into your morning or evening prayers
or added before or after praying to extend the benefits
as you see fit.

this prayerful stretching is an offering back
of the temporal self to the One who created it.
if you can pray while stretching, why not stretch while praying?

choose the physical stretches that work for you.
begin with one or two, add more if you wish
or choose not to stretch . . . this is your own chosen discipline.

stretching God-given muscles and tendons
strengthens the body and offers flexibility to your day
an alternative to yoga, with its embedded spiritual influences.

your suppled body
will love this personal attention built into every day.
it will eagerly await tomorrow's time of prayer.

soul.

invisible, unmeasurable
the eternal element of yourself
worth pampering, worth investing in.

with keen awareness, we feed our bodies three times a day.
how often do we feed our souls?

soul completes the trinity of self
mind . . . body . . . soul

a reflection of the Holy Trinity
Father . . . Son . . . Holy Spirit.

like the object, the light, and the warmth of the sun
three in one.

illumine your daily life by feeding the soul
with prayer and moments of stillness.
this nourished soul will expand to fill the empty spaces
allowing openings for the gentle nudge of the Holy Spirit.

in this world of many demands
allowing time to dwell with God
can become a refuge for soul-nourishment.

purification.

the spa has offered therapeutic baths
for healing and purification
from ancient greece to modern times.

prayer is a preparation of your interior well
to receive God's gift of grace, and to offer living water
from an abundant source to those around you.

just as the evaporation phase purifies water
before replenishing the land with fresh rain

this daily cleansing
this offering up
is a sacred circling of self.

prayer can also be a kind of spiritual breathing
a participation in the breath of the Holy Spirit
an invisible circulation of holiness.

can you imagine the benefits
of a lifetime spent in the prayer spa?

you may end up as that 100-year-old wise one
whose heart knows the depths of prayer intimately
whose life is an outpouring of blessings to all around
and who can drop down and touch toes at a moment's notice!

two

the five senses

celebrate the sensory beauty of holiness

"beauty will save the world."

—fyodor dostoyevsky

when you pray
immerse yourself
in the sensory world God has gifted you.

relish the bodily pleasure of attending to prayer.

discover a new sense of place
as you establish your own prayer corner.

curate this space in your home
where you can be still
where you can focus
where you can be with your Beloved.

anticipate with pleasure stepping
into your sacred space
anticipate dwelling there with Christ.

see.

establish your prayer corner.

celebrate beauty there
with a bit of glimmer, color, candlelight
you have gathered
each day when you arrive to pray.

assemble your chosen components
on the corner of a cabinet or table
a small shelf attached to the wall
a closet or windowsill
where you can stand facing east, if possible.

you may bring:
- an icon of Christ or a saint you admire
- a vessel for charred matches
- a photo of a departed loved one
- a decorative incense burner
- an artful object

when you come to prayer
pause to enjoy this visual
assemblage you have gathered.

when you happen to pass by
you will unexpectedly be surprised
by the beauty of this sacred space
and remember to honor the Inventor of beauty.

smell.

anoint your prayer corner.

release an essential oil or favorite scent
dab frankincense or rose oil on your wrists
and breathe in the luxurious aromas that surround you
each day when you arrive to pray.

enliven your space as you strike the match.
light your candle
and remember that you are a light shining in darkness.

you may bring:
- incense
- a scented candle
- essential oil or fragrance
- a cup of aromatic tea
- fresh flowers

our sense of smell can both humble us
when compared to the keen senses of the animal kingdom
and remind us of our true citizenship
in the Kingdom of God.

like holy chrism contained in a jar
prayers centered in the heart attract divine grace.

like the wise men, offer a sweet-smelling sacrifice
to the King of Kings.

taste.

be refreshed in your prayer corner.

taste and see that the Lord is good.
bring a cup of something delicious
to sip as you pray.

be grateful for the multiple facets of
awareness you have been given.

you may bring:
- an awakening cup of coffee
- something sweet
- a tasty vitamin
- holy water
- a chilled glass of lemon water

by enticing your senses each time you approach prayer
by enjoying the sensation of the cup on your lips
you build patterns of desire with positive messaging.
what better way to use the gifts God has given?

say your morning prayers before a full meal, if possible
to place God before self, and to increase attentiveness.

tell yourself every morning that you look
forward to the nourishing treatment of prayer
that you cannot truly live without it.

hear.

tune your ears to heaven in your prayer corner.

speak or sing your prayers out loud.
they will enter not only into your heart
but through your ears into your mind.

you may bring:
- scriptures
- holy readings
- sacred music
- open windows for bird song
- your own voice in prayer and song

memorize prayers and psalms
nurture mental recall to invigorate your brain cells
and construct an internal resource containing truth.

imagine Christ's presence constantly at your prayer corner
inviting you to join Him, to pause for a moment
each time you walk by.

there is a deep satisfaction
in moving through these holy words
that you hold inside you.

enfold a listening pause into your prayers.
listen, not for words
but for the presence of God within your heart.

touch.

feel the textures of your prayer corner.

approach your prayer corner with humility.
fall down in prostration, touching your head or hand to the ground
you are entering the presence of God.

you may bring:
- a prayer rope
- soft socks or slippers
- head scarf
- fragrant lotion
- book of prayers or prayer cards

soothe your skin with scented lotion
recall the alabaster jar of mary's anointing Christ.

connect your body and soul with fingertips
as you make the sign of the cross
an embodied prayer.

sense the weight of your prayer book in hand.
reach for your prayer rope and feel each knot.

if you sit, establish your space with a chair you love.
if you stand, connect with the earth beneath your feet.
you are standing on holy ground

you may wish to remove your shoes.

refreshment.

prayer attracts God's grace.

establishing this sacred space
is an act of co-creation with God
an agreement that the created world is good.

speak to God freely, in your own words
during your daily prayers, or at any time
tell Him all that is on your mind.

ask God to help you to pray
place your strong will into his tender embrace.

if even one person truly prays
it may serve the whole family, the whole community
the whole world.

there is a thin veil between earth and heaven.
acquiring the temporal habit of prayer
is a solid investment in the well-being of your soul
both now and in the age to come.

prayer is a way toward theosis—union with God
sharing in His divine nature, through grace.
this is a long, narrow pathway
which must be sought after with great humility and perseverance.

yet spiritual refreshment is available to any person
who wishes to partake in the tangible beauty
of a life seeking the Holy in this grace-infused world.

three

your prayer plan

honor this appointment, lift your face toward God

"make peace with yourself, and both
heaven and earth will make peace with you."

—saint isaac the syrian

as a daily treatment for the soul
a prayer plan is tailored to your personal needs.

early christians called this a prayer rule
used to organize their prayers each day.

the three main elements of spoken prayer are
praising God
thanking God
asking God.

mornings and evenings are often the best times for this treatment.
you determine the raw materials
you set the appointment
you honor the time.

this daily act of love is simply
a disciplined turning back to God, and all He has given us
to gradually increase His eternal Kingdom within our hearts.
this brings peace which surpasses understanding.

schedule.

determine to commit yourself to prayer every day.
enfold your life into the life of Christ
for the temporal and eternal benefits.

start with ten minutes once a day
plus one additional pause at your prayer corner
for a mini detox
. . . a holy pause, a word of gratitude, a concern, a psalm.

at your chosen time of prayer, you may:
- pause for a moment of silence
- recall the order of your prayer plan
- offer written or memorized prayers
- speak your own concerns
- be still and know that he is God

you may decide to choose an alternative prayer plan
for sunday mornings before church, for a special treat.

at the beginning, you must force yourself to pray
but soon, prayer becomes essential to a day well lived.

if prayer is cut short one day
don't worry, just resolve to allow a generous time tomorrow.

there are twenty-four hours in a day, all given to us by God.
finding the time may seem difficult at first
but once you decide, you can see it is a small sacrifice
like arising a few minutes early to prepare your cup of coffee.

the first fruits of morning are perfect
before the cares of the day carry you away.
typically, there is a 5:50 to 6:00 a.m. opening
in most people's schedule. . . .

commitment.

building on this relationship means spending time together
pressing past the mental block
that either God is too overwhelming to approach
or that the small things of life are more demanding
than He who holds the universe in His hands.

begin simply, and extend the conversation as you are ready.
feel the words of prayer in your heart.
remember, fewer words, focused intently
are better than many.

make a list of daily prayers you have chosen.
you can write this prayer plan down on paper
or on the prayer card given on page 97.
a pencil is helpful to allow for adjustments as you progress.

remembering your own prayer plan
or memorizing a verse of scripture or a psalm
may take time—this is therapy for the mind and soul.
consider it time well spent with the One you love.

time, which normally flies, can slow during prayer
creating a temptation to curtail your session early.
instead, keep your allotted time frame, slowing the pace.

dwelling in close relationship with God
does not come about just by wishing for it.
you must commit yourself firmly to this daily task.

anticipate each soothing session with joy and longing. . . .
over time, yours will soon become a life built on prayer.

praising.

throughout time, lovers of God
cannot help crying out their prayers of praise.

you can see this in the centuries-old
psalms and songs of king david to his Lord.

your prayer plan can be a combination
of holy prayers, thoughts that arise in you
memorized wisdom, and scriptures.

choose words and songs and hymns of praise
that make your own heart sing.
offer yourself to Christ with love.

by imprinting these words on your heart
these words of doxology, of praise
spoken, chanted, or lifted up in song
you learn to know God on a deeper level.

in a world where praise for self is pervasive
we must remember Who is worthy
Who has given us such a gift . . .
the possibility of spending eternal life in joy
dwelling with God.

we can actually join our voices
with the ongoing hymns of the angels
a collective song of praise spanning the created order
a collaboration of heaven and earth—
holy, holy, holy art Thou, o God!

thanking.

construct a daily mindset filled with giving thanks
to focus on blessings you have received.

keep a gratitude list
in your mind and on paper
to dwell on the people and the things
God has placed in your path . . . near and far, large and small.

when God answers prayers
when He works in your life
do not allow yourself to forget this divine intervention
write it down in your prayer journal, and remember.

if we believe that all Good comes from God
why not lift your face with thankful glances
a hundred times a day?

standing at your prayer corner
be still, take a deep, intentional breath
and thank God for this breath.

you can offer the whole body gratitudes (page 87)
as you give thanks for your:
steady breath
beating heart
walking feet
working hands
God-given mind
God-seeking soul

each numbered day we are given to live on this earth is a gift.
don't forget to say thank you.

asking.

your gratitude list
may overlap with your list of petitions
for your family, home, work
for the beauty and the pain we see on planet earth.

this is natural.
just lift this all up to your Father in heaven
who needs no instruction on what to do.

when people you know of are in need
you can spontaneously offer their concerns to the Creator of all
or write their names on your list of petitions
and pray for them daily.

you can also raise your voice in song
and offer special prayers for the departed
especially for the first forty days after their repose.
they are really just a thin veil away. . . .

fear, anxiety, worry, impatience, resentfulness, anger
these can be crippling.
ask your Father in heaven to comfort you.

by asking for forgiveness when you fall short
you can practice humility and focus on the true.

love God . . . love neighbor,
and trust that all works together for good to those who love.

alignment.

you can design your prayer plan
to align the work of feeding your own soul.
as you grow in prayer, this routine can change and grow with you.

in two months a new habit can be set.
once established, this sacred space in time and place
will become a core building block in your day
like a nutritious meal, or daily connection with a person you love.

if life interrupts your prayer plan
don't worry
just seize the next chance
to drench yourself in prayer once again.

if you sense spiritual cooling for a time
just keep showing up, even for a brief session.
the desert and the garden are both a part of the Kingdom of God.

if you belong to a worshiping community
you may receive strength there.
your priest or spiritual mentor can offer direction
from holy wisdom of the centuries to guide your prayer plan.

the church can be a hospital for the soul
with her prescriptions for temporal and eternal healing.
partake of the healing medicine that is offered there
like fasting before prayer, for lightness of being.
allow hunger pangs in your day to bring remembrance of God.

as you praise God, thank God, and ask God for help
you align yourself to the divine will
and remember your own place as His beloved child.

four

inner stillness

dwell in your deep heart

"the heart of the matter is:
stand with reverence before God,
with the mind in the heart,
and strive toward him with longing."

—saint theophan the recluse

to dwell in this place of inner stillness requires training
centering the reaches of your mind
warming the "*nous*"—the spiritual center of your intellect.

this interior action
invisible to the eye
is numinous
intimate
intense
alive.

don't be surprised
if you need to remove your sweater
as your soul senses the presence of the Holy Spirit
as your body warms with the interior glow of silent prayer
as you dwell with God.

focus.

you are the attendant to your own soul.
to gain the inner stillness that leads to depth of prayer
you must prepare the right conditions.

inner stillness does not exist in a void.
focused prayer centers our mind on God
allows our deep heart to expand.

slowing the pace can help your concentration.
a small movement may be of service
raising hands, lowering head, slowing breath
or simply pause, connect, then continue.

distracting thoughts will attempt to enter your mind.
do not worry about this, also do not engage them.
do not punish yourself, but simply move forward.

these thoughts are just chattering sparrows
do not let them land in your branches
but dismiss them, redouble your efforts
and gently draw your mind into your heart again and again.

while we are not seeking emotional experience
or forming visual images in our minds
the presence of God is often palpable in the stillness.

pierce your own heart with focused love for God
until it begins to ache, feeling His presence.
this grace-filled state may bring a sense of
physical warmth, heart swelling, or tears.

these brief moments are a gift of grace God may offer
to the deeply seeking soul, if and when the conditions are ripe.

mercy.

passed down from centuries of christian luminaries
the Jesus Prayer is a very personal calling upon the name of Jesus
a cry of hope to the name which is above every name
to the name which upholds the entire universe.

bow your head, close your eyes, descend your mind
into the very center of your heart, and hold it there, firmly.

focus on the inner sense of Christ's presence
then speak these words to Him, with love.

Lord Jesus Christ, have mercy on me.
Lord Jesus Christ, have mercy on me.
Lord Jesus Christ, have mercy on me.

when you say, "Lord Jesus Christ"
understand that all Good derives from Him.
when you say, "have mercy on me"
be assured that you are His precious child.

kyrie eleison is the greek translation for "Lord, have mercy."
kyrie means "Lord," while "mercy" is derived from *eleos*
an image of soothing, healing oil poured over the head as pure grace.

the beloved Jesus Prayer, in its radical simplicity
sums up the whole gospel.
the incarnation, the sovereignty of Christ, and our very salvation are all there.

it confirms the Holy Trinity, with Jesus known
as Son of the Father, while praying by illumination of the Holy Spirit.

placing our trust in His boundless wisdom and care for us
is not a desperate plea for mercy, to escape judgment
but an affirmation of God's healing power in our lives.

attend.

time presses upon us
leading us to believe the pressure never ends.
the Jesus Prayer can be an antidote to this perception.

you can pray as you move through the day
or you can intentionally walk, sit, or awaken early just to pray.

you may recall the Jesus Prayer when you:
- are still or moving
- are worried
- are filled with gratitude
- lay your head down
- awake from sleep

standing before the Lord is the most attentive position
you may also choose to sit quietly.
these prayers may be said aloud, in a whisper, or in silence.

do not bring visual images of Christ into your imagination
but stand before the living God with an inner sense of His presence
and the potent name of Jesus on your lips.

if you pray without attentiveness, there will be no fruit.
if you seek delight in God, you will find your joy.

as you progress, you may wish to match your breathing to this rhythm
this should only be practiced
with an experienced spiritual father or mother.

as you speak this prayer to Christ
allow yourself to dwell with Him
allow yourself to dwell in Love.

continuous.

the Jesus Prayer is a gift of the desert monastic tradition
a simple way to pray without ceasing.

strive to nurture the conditions of ceaseless prayer
by keeping the constant presence of the living Christ
on your lips, in your mind, in your heart.

this is an interior force toward the positive.
rather than emptying our minds, we fill them with Christ.

saint paul believed that continuous prayer is possible
and so prescribed it in his letters to four of his communities
the romans, ephesians, colossians, and thessalonians.

to approach ceaseless prayer, dwell not in the mind but in the heart
listen to the wordless voice of God within you
allow grace to permeate your being.

this method of contemplative prayer relies on our own efforts
in cooperation with the indwelling of the Holy Spirit.
remember, this is a relationship.

with time and much perseverance
God may one day gift you with self-acting "prayer of the heart"
the name of Jesus continuously flowing inside you.
when granted, this is indeed a rare foretaste of heaven.

ceaseless prayer holds the power of so deep a consolation
as you mystically unite yourself to Christ.

meanwhile, do the hard work of being still and receiving.
little by little you can train your mind to descend into your heart
and to dwell with God in every moment.
this positive, alert, listening silence is called *hesychia*.

by carrying God's presence deep in the center of your heart
you may one day become, through grace
a person who has been turned into prayer.

being.

life carries us forward, fast.
yet for those who are listening
the human spirit yearns toward the still center
where we encounter God.

not a distant God, but an intimate Comforter
closer than we can even know.

while our lives are often immersed in the pursuit of material things
there are slender openings we can train our hearts to enter into.

father anthony bloom taught a method
for gathering the crumbs of wasted time
and transforming them into something holy.

the secret of this contemplative exercise is to find joy
simply being with God
as you listen for His voiceless presence within your heart.

an exercise in stillness:
- sit or stand quietly
- set an alarm for three minutes
- say to God, "here i am"
- do nothing . . . just be . . .
- rest in the presence of God

real silence has a density
in the intersection of eternity with time.
at the heart of the silence, God can be found
a divine presence filled with peace.

be silent; be attentive to the wordless presence of God within your own heart.

remember, you are a human being, not a human doing —a child of God.

intention.

prayer is intimacy with God
and contemplation of the invisible
as saint gregory of nyssa tells us.

while inner stillness is rare in this age of incessant noise
it is not difficult to cultivate the interior life.
it merely requires intentionally placing God before self over time.

you are teaching your mind to be quiet
and your whole heart to be filled with love
establishing a haven where you can always find Christ.

when you pray the Jesus Prayer, remember:
- descend your mind into your heart
- feel the words of your prayer there
- focus on the name of Jesus
- train your mind to deny distracting thoughts
- speak the name of your Lord with love

once you have established
an intimate prayer room inside your heart
layer the walls with prayer until it is well-formed.

after this, you will have an interior retreat you may enter anytime
to warm your soul with the prayers of inner stillness
to sense the peace of dwelling with God.

as we train our minds to be still
we may begin to perceive the substance of silence.

five

an offering

offer the world back as sacrament

"homo adorans. the first and basic definition of man
is that he is the priest. he stands at the center of the world
and unifies it in his act of blessing God,
of both receiving the world from God
and offering it to God. . . ."

—father alexander schmemann

we are all part of a lavish mosaic
as members of the priesthood of all believers.

before we can begin to offer EVERYTHING back
that we have freely received on this beautiful planet earth
we must first come to the realization
that our soul is in exile in a strange land.

but once we embrace the tangible gifts
we have been given in this God-infused world
that every created thing can be a sign of His presence
that everywhere we look, we may find Christ.

we can offer the elements placed before us back to their Creator
as sacraments of the Kingdom of God.

transformation.

in the garden, we began.
we were placed there
not only to think thoughts (as *homo sapiens*)
or to make things (as *homo faber*)
but first, to worship God (as *homo adorans*).

it is a question of pride versus humility
found at the root of many choices.

we are in a unique position
both eternal as the angelic order
and material as the natural order.

as creative beings
we are made in the image of God, the Creator
yet we, ourselves, make nothing *ex nihilo*.

but gathering the matter given to us
water, flowers, vegetables, animals, image, color . . .
all of creation can become sacrament
a visible sign of divine grace.

we can transform the gifts of our hands into offerings
to the Creator of all, honoring Him with our daily actions
with minds set on spiritual growth
bodies poised to support this movement within us
and souls ever expanding with the oblation of our lives.

as worshiping beings, we are to remember the garden
and honor the One who fashioned us there
transforming the material world placed before us
into something holy, as another way to worship God.

encircle.

a fourth-century aid to contemplative prayer
the christian prayer rope is a way to offer time
kairos time, in the moment . . . not chronos time, by the clock.

traditionally it is tied with knots made of nine crosses
one cross representing each order of the angels.

to use the prayer rope, simply repeat the Jesus Prayer
while moving from knot to knot with the thumb and forefinger
as you circle the rope forward with your left hand, saying

Lord Jesus Christ, have mercy on me.
Lord Jesus Christ, have mercy on me.
Lord Jesus Christ, have mercy on me.

you may simultaneously make the sign of the cross with right hand
touch forehead, center of chest, right then left shoulders.
use thumb and first two fingertips together, representing the Holy Trinity
keep last two fingertips pressed to palm
representing the two natures of Christ.

bowing your head, you may form a kind of circle
with your upper body, to help your mind descend into your heart.

begin with a short prayer rope of thirty-three knots
which you may encircle once as you pray the Jesus Prayer
or as you pray for your concerns.

increase to two, then three times around.
progress to a long prayer rope of 100 knots if you wish.

these may be found at orthodox church bookstores or online
a useful tool for growing in prayer.

retreat.

an oasis in time can materialize
by insisting on an annual personal prayer retreat.

discover a monastery, guest house, or quiet room
within your range—any secluded space will suffice—
and treat yourself to 24–48 hours of cloistered retreat.

this is a solitary ritual for you and God alone
a time to pray, to journal, to rest
to read spiritual books, to quiet your mind
to consider the year behind you and the year ahead.

you may wish to assemble a traveling prayer kit
in a small box or pouch, and gather a few holy items
to support your traveling sanctuary.

you may bring:
- a small icon
- a prayer rope
- a prayer book or cards
- a travel candle
- an adornment of beauty

this prayer kit can travel with you on any trip
inviting remembrance of God
as you begin or end each bustling day.

this is also a way to love your neighbor
by prioritizing your own relationship to God.

an act of faith can bring ripples of grace throughout the cosmos
while refilling your own well, as you dwell with your Beloved.

return.

our daily prayer plan may unravel at times.
disruptions in our lives may interrupt our routine.
outside forces may pull us away.

to return to your own heart's desire
takes a force of will.

once you realize you are standing at a distance
don't allow defeating thoughts to arise
but forgive your own absence
and simply turn back to the One you love.

begin with a short session, or mini detox.
a mini detox can take many forms
it can serve to gently lift you back to your proper place
resting in the buoyant peace of God.

mini detox:
- relish the act of lighting your candle
- rest a moment in stillness
- say to God, "help me to desire to pray"
- lift up one concern, one gratitude to God
- melt into one favorite stretch

restart your daily routine with a short visit
plan to lengthen your session tomorrow.

remember your truest love
the One who created you from nothing
the One who created you for intimacy with Him.

consider.

don't rush prayer.
a few prayers thoughtfully spoken
are better than racing through too many.
allow room for your desire to grow.

as with a physical workout regime
begin with a little, and increase as you are ready.

pause to hold in your heart for a moment
each person or thing you present before God.

if asked for your cloak, give your tunic also.
if asked for a moment of your time, give more than a moment.

now modern devices, which we use for so many things
can help us in our prayer life.

you may consider:
- setting alarm to awaken early
- glancing at clock to mark silent prayer
- ringtone reminders for praying the hours
- photos of scriptures and psalms for memorization
- daily prayer apps for ongoing connection

as internal order becomes established in your soul
you may find a new kind of peace in your daily life.

pray with warmth, allow every word to reach your heart.
being attentive within this lengthening of time
is an offering of love.

if you pray without attentiveness, there will be no fruit.
if you seek delight in God, you will find your joy.

remember.

miraculously, as worshiping beings confined in time
we have been given the treasure of each hour, of each day
as long as we have breath.

we can seize this opportunity to align our soul and body
in preparation for our next great adventure, eternal life.

visual reminders help.
keep a prayer rope in your car
a cross at your workplace
an icon in your daily path.

it may take months to learn a psalm
as you build neural pathways toward God.
consider it time well spent with the One you love.

to memorize a psalm:
- repeat it daily
- dig into the meaning
- write it down
- gradually remove the written text
- take the psalm inside you

as the psalmists remind us
the Lord is pleased with a sacrifice of righteousness.

as we sanctify our time
as we begin to unite ourselves with Christ
we may offer those around us a glimpse of heaven.

we may offer back to God
the portion of eternity that He has placed before us
in this singular life we have been gifted.

we may offer back our very selves.

six

the hours

transform time into prayer

"i look at Him and He looks at me,
and we are happy together."

—saint john vianney

as creatures contained in time, we can sanctify our days
and savor the remembrance of God
by praying "the hours."

the "major hours" consist of morning and evening prayers.

you may choose to expand your offering to include
the seven "divine services" throughout the day
spoken on their designated hour, or adjusted to fit your schedule.

medieval church bells, rooted in jewish tradition,
would ring to call christians to prayer throughout the day.

on this swiftly tilting planet
where humans have fallen down before their Creator
century after century, in awe . . .
at times this "enlightened" society seems to have forgotten God.

praying the hours is an antidote to this forgetful world.

praying the hours.

to celebrate each divine service
you may choose to meditate upon the theme
or to speak the designated psalms as you pray the hours.

1st Hour • 6 am • psalm 5
Christ, the true light of the world
my voice shalt Thou hear in the morning, o Lord.

3rd Hour • 9 am • psalm 50 (51)
descent of the Holy Spirit
create in me a clean heart, o God
and renew a right spirit within me.

6th Hour • 12 noon • psalm 53 (54)
Christ ascends the cross
i will praise Thy name, o Lord, for it is good.

9th Hour • 3 pm • psalm 83 (84)
Christ finishes the work of salvation
blessed are they that dwell in Thy house.

vespers • 6 pm • psalm 140 (141)
gratitude for the blessings of the day
let my prayer be set forth before Thee as incense.

compline • 9 pm • psalm 69 (70)
trust God in sleep and in death
o God, thou art my help and my deliverer.

midnight service • psalm 133 (134)
prepare, the Bridegroom cometh
lift up your hands in the sanctuary, and bless the Lord.

anticipate.

anticipate the next hour
as you might anticipate your next meal
to help you remember God throughout the day
and to transform time into prayer.

you may set a quiet alarm for each hour
to remind you of this holy work.

a verse from the following psalms
or the entire psalm noted may be prayed for each divine service.

orthodox bibles use the septuagint greek translation of the old testament
following the apostles and evangelists who cite it in the new testament.
these psalms retain the lower chapter numbers noted.

this sanctification of self is a gift you can offer to God
to yourself, and to those whose lives you may touch
as your very human nature is transformed.

if you have children, let them catch you praying.
share these short remembrances of God with them.
let them discover your own yearning for prayer
as a treat you quietly prioritize each day.
remember, you too are a child of God, beloved.

as saint john the baptist reminds us
Christ must increase, and we must decrease.

the greatest commandment
is to love God with all your heart, mind, and soul.
praying the hours is one tangible way to act upon this love.

psalms for praying the hours.

1st Hour • 6 am • psalm 5
Christ, the true light of the world

give ear to my words, o Lord, consider my meditation.

hearken unto the voice of my cry, my King, and my God:
for unto thee will i pray.

my voice shalt thou hear in the morning, o Lord;

in the morning will i direct my prayer unto thee, and will look up.

for thou art not a God that hath pleasure in wickedness:
neither shall evil dwell with thee.

the foolish shall not stand in thy sight:
thou hatest all workers of iniquity.

Thou shalt destroy them that speak leasing:
the Lord will abhor the bloody and deceitful man.

but as for me, i will come into thy house in the multitude of thy mercy:
and in thy fear will i worship toward thy holy temple.

lead me, o Lord, in thy righteousness because of mine enemies;
make thy way straight before my face.

for there is no faithfulness in their mouth;
their inward part is very wickedness;
their throat is an open sepulchre; they flatter with their tongue.

destroy thou them, o God; let them fall by their own counsels;
cast them out in the multitude of their transgressions;
for they have rebelled against thee.

but let all those that put their trust in thee rejoice:
let them ever shout for joy, because thou defendest them:
let them also that love thy name be joyful in thee.

for thou, Lord, wilt bless the righteous;
with favor wilt thou compass him as with a shield.

also psalms 89/90, 100/101

3rd hour • 9 am • psalm 50/51
descent of the Holy Spirit

have mercy upon me, o God, according to thy lovingkindness:
according unto the multitude of thy tender mercies
blot out my transgressions.

wash me thoroughly from mine iniquity
and cleanse me from my sin.

for i acknowledge my transgressions: and my sin is ever before me.

against thee, thee only, have i sinned, and done this evil in thy sight:
that thou mightest be justified when thou speakest
and be clear when thou judgest.

behold, i was shapen in iniquity;
and in sin did my mother conceive me.

behold, thou desirest truth in the inward parts:
and in the hidden part thou shalt make me to know wisdom.

purge me with hyssop, and i shall be clean:
wash me, and i shall be whiter than snow.

make me to hear joy and gladness;
that the bones which thou hast broken may rejoice.

hide thy face from my sins, and blot out all mine iniquities.

create in me a clean heart, o God;
and renew a right spirit within me.

cast me not away from thy presence;
and take not thy holy spirit from me.

restore unto me the joy of thy salvation;
and uphold me with thy free spirit.

then will i teach transgressors thy ways;
and sinners shall be converted unto thee.

deliver me from bloodguiltiness, o God,
thou God of my salvation:
and my tongue shall sing aloud of thy righteousness.

o Lord, open thou my lips;
and my mouth shall shew forth thy praise.

for thou desirest not sacrifice; else would i give it:
thou delightest not in burnt offering.

the sacrifices of God are a broken spirit:
a broken and a contrite heart, o God thou wilt not despise.

do good in thy good pleasure unto zion:
build thou the walls of jerusalem.

then shalt thou be pleased with the sacrifices of righteousness
with burnt offering and whole burnt offering:
then shall they offer bullocks upon thine altar.

also psalms 16/17, 60/61

6th Hour • 12 noon • psalm 53/54
Christ ascends the cross

save me, o God, by thy name, and judge me by thy strength.

hear my prayer, o God;
give ear to the words of my mouth.

for strangers are risen up against me, and oppressors seek after my soul:
they have not set God before them. selah.

behold, God is mine helper:
the Lord is with them that uphold my soul.

He shall reward evil unto mine enemies:
cut them off in thy truth.

i will freely sacrifice unto thee:

i will praise thy name, o Lord; for it is good.

for he hath delivered me out of all trouble:
and mine eye hath seen his desire upon mine enemies.

also psalms 54/55, 90/91

9th Hour • 3 pm • psalm 83/84
Christ finishes the work of salvation

how amiable are thy tabernacles
o Lord of hosts!

my soul longeth, yea, even fainteth for the courts of the Lord:
my heart and my flesh crieth out for the living God.

yea, the sparrow hath found an house
and the swallow a nest for herself
where she may lay her young
even thine altars
o Lord of hosts, my King, and my God.

blessed are they that dwell in Thy house:
they will be still praising thee. selah.

blessed is the man whose strength is in thee;
in whose heart are the ways of them.

who passing through the valley of baca make it a well;
the rain also filleth the pools.

they go from strength to strength
every one of them in zion appeareth before God.

o Lord God of hosts, hear my prayer:
give ear, o God of jacob. selah.

behold, o God our shield
and look upon the face of thine anointed.

for a day in thy courts is better than a thousand.
i had rather be a doorkeeper in the house of my God
than to dwell in the tents of wickedness.

for the Lord God is a sun and shield:
the Lord will give grace and glory:
no good thing will he withhold from them that walk uprightly.

o Lord of hosts
blessed is the man that trusteth in thee.

also psalms 84/85, 85/86

Vespers • 6 pm • psalm 140/141
gratitude for the blessings of the day

Lord, i cry unto thee: make haste unto me;
give ear unto my voice, when i cry unto thee.

let my prayer be set forth before thee as incense;
and the lifting up of my hands as the evening sacrifice.

set a watch, o Lord, before my mouth;
keep the door of my lips.

incline not my heart to any evil thing
to practice wicked works with men that work iniquity:
and let me not eat of their dainties.

let the righteous smite me;
it shall be a kindness:
and let him reprove me;
it shall be an excellent oil, which shall not break my head:
for yet my prayer also shall be in their calamities.

when their judges are overthrown in stony places
they shall hear my words; for they are sweet.

our bones are scattered at the grave's mouth
as when one cutteth and cleaveth wood upon the earth.

but mine eyes are unto thee
o God the Lord: in thee is my trust;
leave not my soul destitute.

keep me from the snares which they have laid for me
and the gins of the workers of iniquity.

let the wicked fall into their own nets
whilst that i withal escape.

also psalms 103/104, 129/30

Compline • 9 pm • psalm 69/70
trust God in sleep and in death

make haste, o God, to deliver me;
make haste to help me, o Lord.

let them be ashamed and confounded
that seek after my soul:
let them be turned backward
and put to confusion, that desire my hurt.

let them be turned back
for a reward of their shame that say, aha, aha.

let all those that seek thee rejoice and be glad in thee:
and let such as love thy salvation say continually
let God be magnified.

but i am poor and needy: make haste unto me
o God: thou art my help and my deliverer;
o Lord, make no tarrying.

also psalms 50/51, 142/3

midnight service • psalm 133/134

prepare, the Bridegroom cometh

behold, bless ye the Lord, all ye servants of the Lord
which by night stand in the house of the Lord.

lift up your hands in the sanctuary, and bless the Lord.

the Lord that made heaven and earth bless thee out of zion.

also psalms 118/119, 120/121

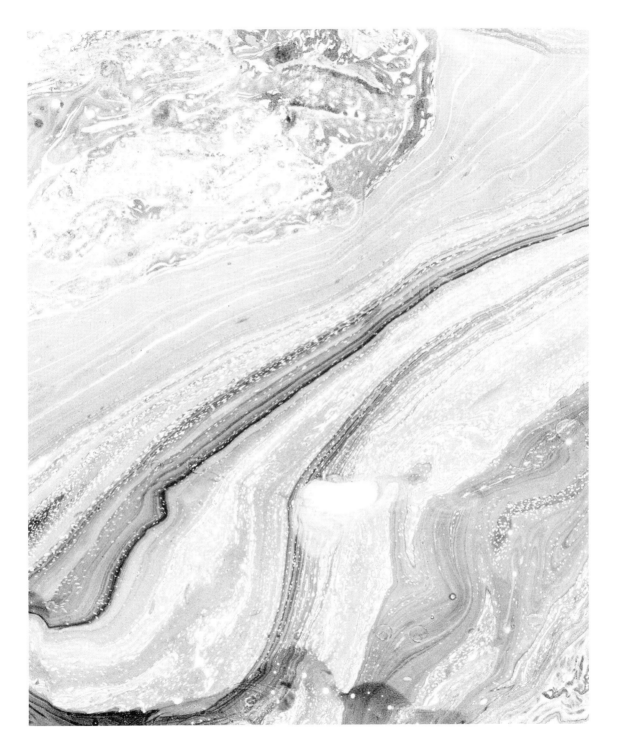

seven

tools for therapy

wrap wisdom from the ages into each day

"i have come home at last! this is my real country! i belong here.
this is the land I have been looking for all my life,
though I never knew it till now. . . . come further up,
come further in!"

—c. s. lewis

following is a small collection of sacred words
that you may choose to wrap into your daily prayer routine.

remember the therapies of the prayer spa:
- honor your mind, body, and soul
- celebrate the five senses given to you
- establish an intentional prayer plan
- warm your heart with inner stillness
- offer back each hour, each day to God

you may open this book daily or commit words to memory
to accompany your own spoken thoughts to God.

you may also add other scriptures, stretches and prayers that you love—
there is such a wide world of wisdom.

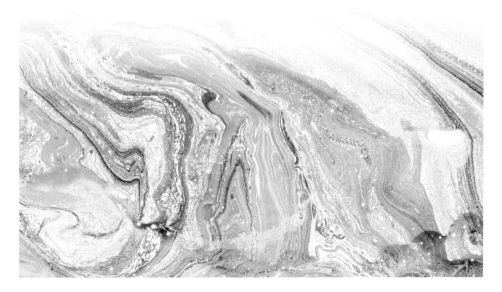

body treatments for the prayer spa.

begin slowly, relax muscles, use gentle movements
feet shoulder-width apart
knees soft, don't forget to breathe, repeat as you wish
stop if there is pain.

orthodox liturgical movements

sign of the cross: with right hand, touch forehead, center of chest, right then left shoulder

hands raised: raise both hands with elbows resting at sides, palms toward you, head bowed

metania: make the sign of the cross, reach toward ground with right hand, then rise

kneeling: on both knees, with upper body upright or draped forward with forehead touching ground

prostration: drop to hands then knees, touch forehead to ground, push upward from hands to rise

alternative movements: standing stretches for daily prayer

neck rotation: rotate head to look over left then right shoulder, hold five seconds each

neck roll: drop chin to chest, roll to right, slightly back, to left, back down, reverse

shoulder roll: arms at side, circle shoulders up, forward, down, backward, up, reverse

contract core: pull navel back to spine, lift pelvic floor muscles, hold five seconds

spine roll: fold down to touch toes, hold, roll each vertebra up to standing

lifted hands: stand tall, clasp hands above head, stretch upward

cross stretch: with lifted hands, slowly bend torso side to side, then slightly back to front, making a kinesthetic cross with your upper body

ascending adorations

whole-body gratitudes

God grant me:

awareness of the presence of God
in every moment
(fold down to touch toes)

attentiveness to my thoughts
(roll up to knees)

acquisition of the Holy Spirit
(roll up to waist)

alignment of body and soul
(roll up to chest)

abiding in Christ
(cross stretch)

spine roll/lifted hands
repeat three times

thank you God, for my:

steady breath
(deep breath)

beating heart
(fold down)

walking feet
(touch toes)

working hands
(roll up to waist)

God-given mind
(roll up to standing)

God-seeking soul
(lifted hands)

spine roll/cross stretch
repeat three times

orthodox prayers for refreshment.

the Jesus Prayer, various versions

Lord Jesus Christ, have mercy on me.
Lord Jesus Christ, have mercy on us.
Lord Jesus Christ, have mercy on (name).
Lord Jesus Christ, Son of God, have mercy on me, a sinner.

byzantine hymn
Kyrie eleison/Lord, have mercy
(can be spoken or sung)

ky-ri-e e-le-i-son ky-ri-e e-le-i-son ky-ri-e e-le-i-son

prayer for the beginning of the day
by saint philaret of moscow

o Lord, grant that i may meet the coming day in peace.
help me in all things to rely upon Thy holy will.
in every hour of the day, reveal Thy will to me.
bless my dealings with all who surround me.
teach me to treat all that comes to me throughout the day
with peace of soul, and with the firm conviction
that Thy will governs all.
in all my deeds and words guide my thoughts and feelings.
in unforseen events, let me not forget that all are sent by Thee.
teach me to act firmly and wisely
without embittering and embarrassing others.
give me the strength to bear the fatigue of the coming day
with all that it shall bring.
direct my will. teach me to pray.
pray Thou Thyself in me.
amen.

morning prayers

in the name of the Father, and of the Son,
and of the Holy Spirit. amen.
glory to Thee, our God, glory to Thee.
Heavenly King, o Comforter, the Spirit of truth
Who art everywhere present and fillest all things
o Treasury of every good and Bestower of life:
come and dwell in us, and cleanse us from every stain
and save our souls, o Good One.

Holy God, Holy Mighty, Holy Immortal, have mercy on us. (3)

glory to the Father, and to the Son, and to the Holy Spirit;
both now and ever, and unto the ages of ages. amen.

All-holy Trinity, have mercy on us.
Lord, be gracious unto our sins. Master, pardon our iniquities.
Holy One, visit and heal our infirmities for Thy name's sake.

Lord, have mercy. (3)

glory to the Father, and to the Son, and to the Holy Spirit;
both now and ever, and unto the ages of ages. Amen.

our Father, Which art in the heavens, hallowed be Thy name.
Thy Kingdom come. Thy will be done, on earth as it is in heaven.
give us this day our daily bread. and forgive us our debts
as we forgive our debtors. and lead us not into temptation
but deliver us from the evil one.

through the prayers of our holy Fathers
Lord Jesus Christ our God, have mercy on us. amen.

morning prayers 2

Troparia to the Holy Trinity:

as we arise from sleep, we fall down before Thee, o Good One
and we cry unto Thee with the hymn of the angels, o Mighty One:
holy, holy, holy art Thou, o God. through the Theotokos, have mercy on us.

glory to the Father, and to the Son, and to the Holy Spirit.

having raised me from bed and from sleep, o Lord
enlighten my mind and my heart, and open Thou my lips
that i may praise Thee, o Holy Trinity.
holy, holy, holy art Thou, o God. through the Theotokos, have mercy on us.

both now and ever, and unto the ages of ages. amen.

of a sudden the Judge shall come, and the deeds of each shall be laid bare.
but let us cry out with fear in the midst of the night:
holy, holy, holy art Thou, o God. through the Theotokos, have mercy on us.

Lord, have mercy. (12)

as i rise from sleep i thank Thee, o Holy Trinity
for because of Thy great goodness and long-suffering
Thou wast not wroth with me, the slothful and sinner
nor didst Thou destroy me in mine iniquities
but didst show Thy wonted love for man, and when i was prostrate in despair
Thou didst raise me to keep the morning watch and glorify Thy dominion.
and now enlighten Thou the eyes of my mind
open my mouth to meditate on Thy words and to understand Thy commandments
and to do Thy will, and to chant unto Thee in heartfelt confession
and praise Thine all-holy name, of the Father, and of the Son, and of the Holy Spirit
now and ever, and unto the ages of ages. amen.

o come, let us worship and fall down before our King and God.
o come, let us worship and fall down before Christ, our King and God.
o come, let us worship and fall down before Him, Christ the King and our God.

amen.

through the prayers of our holy fathers
Lord Jesus Christ our God, have mercy on us. amen.
glory to Thee, our God, glory to Thee.
Heavenly King, o Comforter, the Spirit of truth, Who art everywhere present and
fillest all things, o Treasury of every good and Bestower of life:
come and dwell in us, and cleanse us from every stain, and save our souls
o Good One.

Holy God, Holy Mighty, Holy Immortal, have mercy on us. (3)

glory to the Father, and to the Son, and to the Holy Spirit; both now and ever
and unto the ages of ages. amen.

All-holy Trinity, have mercy on us.
Lord, be gracious unto our sins. Master, pardon our iniquities.
Holy One, visit and heal our infirmities for Thy name's sake.

Lord, have mercy. (12)

glory to the Father, and to the Son, and to the Holy Spirit;
both now and ever, and unto the ages of ages. amen.

o come, let us worship and fall down before our King and God.
o come, let us worship and fall down before Christ, our King and God.
o come, let us worship and fall down before Him, Christ the King and our God.
amen.

(psalm 50/51 may also be prayed as an evening prayer.)

psalm 50 (51)

have mercy on me, o God, according to Thy great mercy;
and according to the multitude of Thy compassions
blot out my transgression.
wash me thoroughly from mine iniquity
and cleanse me from my sin.
for i know mine iniquity, and my sin is ever before me.
against Thee only have i sinned and done this evil before Thee
that Thou mightest be justified in Thy words
and prevail when Thou art judged.
for behold, i was conceived in iniquities
and in sins did my mother bear me.
for behold, Thou hast loved truth;
the hidden and secret things of Thy wisdom
hast Thou made manifest unto me.
Thou shalt sprinkle me with hyssop, and i shall be made clean;
thou shalt wash me, and i shall be made whiter than snow.
Thou shalt make me to hear joy and gladness;
the bones that be humbled, they shall rejoice.
turn thy face away from my sins, and blot out all mine iniquities.
create in me a clean heart, o God, and renew a right spirit within me.
cast me not away from Thy presence
and take not Thy Holy Spirit from me.
restore unto me the joy of Thy salvation
and with Thy governing Spirit establish me.
i shall teach transgressors Thy ways
and the ungodly shall turn back unto Thee.
deliver me from blood-guiltiness, o God, Thou God of my salvation;
my tongue shall rejoice in Thy righteousness.
o Lord, Thou shalt open my lips, and my mouth shall declare Thy
praise.

for if Thou hadst desired sacrifice, i had given it;
with whole-burnt offerings Thou shalt not be pleased.
a sacrifice unto God is a broken spirit;
a heart that is broken and humbled God will not despise.
do good, o Lord, in Thy good pleasure unto sion
and let the walls of Jerusalem be builded.
then shalt Thou be pleased with a sacrifice of righteousness
with oblation and whole-burnt offerings.
then shall they offer bullocks upon Thine altar.

morning and evening prayers excerpted from a prayer book for orthodox
christians, by holy transfiguration monastery.

prayer cards for daily plan

sample prayer plan

✠

MY DAILY PRAYERS

(3 prostrations)
"here i am"

morning prayers
(metanias)
sing kyrie eleison ×3
prayer for the beginning of the day

gratitude
petitions

"prayer is intimacy with god
and contemplation of the invisible"
Jesus prayer

listening pause
(hands raised)

GRATITUDE	PETITIONS
deep breath	(shoulder roll)
	julia
whole body	mark
gratitudes	sarah
(spine roll / lifted hands)	eva
	johnsons
family circle	marshalls
(kneeling)	smiths
home	our leaders
work	our cities
health	our churches
protection	the world
Kingdom of god	humility
	forgiveness
	(3 prostrations)

your own prayer plan

✠

MY DAILY PRAYERS

_____

_____
_____
_____
_____
_____
_____
_____
_____
_____
_____
_____
_____
_____
_____
_____
_____

GRATITUDE   PETITIONS

_____   _____
_____   _____
_____   _____
_____   _____
_____   _____
_____   _____
_____   _____
_____   _____
_____   _____
_____   _____
_____   _____
_____   _____
_____   _____
_____   _____
_____   _____
_____   _____
_____   _____
_____   _____
_____   _____
_____   _____
_____   _____

POUSTINIA PRESS

cut and fold at center, and glue back-to-back.
copy this prototype or make your own lists.

supplement 2
scriptures to pray, to memorize

pray without ceasing:
four letters from paul to four communities

" rejoice in your hope, be patient in tribulation, be constant in prayer."
   —romans 12:12

" pray at all times in the Spirit, with all prayer and supplication.
   to that end keep alert with all perseverance, making supplication
   for all the saints."
   —ephesians 6:18

" continue steadfastly in prayer, being watchful in it with thanksgiving."
   —colossians 4:2

" pray constantly, give thanks in all circumstances;
   for this is the will of God in Christ Jesus for you."
   —1 thessalonians 5:17–18

praying the hours

" seven times a day i praise thee for thy righteous ordinances."
  —psalm 119:164

" and it was the third hour, when they crucified him.
  and the inscription of the charge against him read
  'the King of the Jews.' and with him they crucified two robbers
  one on his right and one on his left."
  —mark 15:25–27

" now peter and john were going up to the temple at the hour of prayer
  the ninth hour."
  —acts 3:1

" four days ago, about this hour
  I was keeping the ninth hour of prayer in my house;
  and behold, a man stood before me in bright apparel, saying
  'cornelius, your prayer has been heard
  and your alms have been remembered before God.'"
  —acts 10:30–31

" but about midnight paul and silas were praying and singing hymns to God
  and the prisoners were listening to them."
  —acts 16:25

the Jesus Prayer in scripture

" and he cried, 'Jesus, Son of David, have mercy on me!'
  and those who were in front rebuked him, telling him to be silent;
  but he cried out all the more, 'Son of David, have mercy on me!'"
  —luke 18:38–39

additional verses referencing the Jesus Prayer:

matthew 9:27; 15:22; 17:15; 20:30–31;   luke 17:13;
mark 10:47–48;   psalm 50 (51)

favorite verses to remember

" i appeal to you therefore, brethren, by the mercies of God
   to present your bodies as a living sacrifice, holy and acceptable to God
   which is your spiritual worship. do not be conformed to this world
   but be transformed by the renewal of your mind."
   —romans 12:1–2

" rejoice in the Lord always; again i will say, rejoice.
   let all men know your forbearance.
   the Lord is at hand. have no anxiety about anything
   but in everything by prayer and supplication with thanksgiving
   let your requests be made known to God.
   and the peace of God, which passes all understanding
   will keep your hearts and your minds in Christ Jesus."
   —philippians 4:4–7

" trust in the Lord with all your heart, and do not rely on your own insight.
   in all your ways acknowledge him, and he will make straight your paths."
   —proverbs 3:5–6

" let us then with confidence draw near to the throne of grace
   that we may receive mercy and find grace to help in time of need."
   —hebrews 4:16

" but when you pray, go into your room and shut the door
   and pray to your Father who is in secret;
   and your Father who sees in secret will reward you."
   —matthew 6:6

" they said to each other, 'did not our hearts burn within us
   while he talked to us on the road, while he opened to us the scriptures?'"
   –luke 24:32

" i desire then that in every place the men should pray
   lifting holy hands without anger or quarreling."
   –1 timothy 2:8

supplement 3
sources for growth

The Way of a Pilgrim, by an anonymous pilgrim
adapted to modern american usage by Faith Annette Sand;
translated from the russian by R.M. French

> " Sometimes by calling upon the name of Jesus I was overwhelmed
> with bliss and now I knew the meaning of the words, *'The Kingdom of
> God is within you.'"*
> (pasadena, ca: hope publishing house, 1993), page 39.

Beginning to Pray, by Metropolitan Anthony Bloom

> " When God breaks through to us or when we break through to God,
> in certain exceptional circumstances . . . when we suddenly discover
> in ourselves a depth where prayer abides and out of which it can gush
> forth, there is no problem of prayer."
> (mahwah, nj: paulist press, 1970), page 25.

Prayer: Encounter with the Living God, by Metropolitan Hilarion Alfeyev

> " Prayer is an encounter with the Living God. Christianity gives man
> direct access to God, who listens to man, helps him, and loves him.
> This is the fundamental difference between Christianity and, for
> example Buddhism, in which during meditation the one praying deals
> with a certain impersonal super-being."
> (yonkers, ny: st. vladimir's seminary press, 2015), page 9.

On Prayer, by Saint John of Kronstadt

> " When you pray, make every effort to feel with your heart the truth
> and power of your prayer, and feed upon these qualities as upon
> imperishable food; saturate your heart with them as with dew; warm
> yourself as by a blessed fire."
> (jordanville, ny: Holy Trinity monastery, 1994), page 7.

The Power of the Name: The Jesus Prayer in Orthodox Spirituality
by Bishop Kallistos of Diokleia

> " Silence is not merely negative–a pause between words, a temporary cessation of speech–but, properly understood, it is highly positive: an attitude of attentive alertness, of vigilance, and above all of *listening*. The *hesychast*, the person who has attained *hesychia*, inner stillness or silence, is *par excellence* the one who listens." (oxford, uk: slg press, 2013), page 1.

The Jesus Prayer:
The Ancient Desert Prayer That Tunes the Heart to God
by Frederica Mathewes-Green

> " As you form the habit of saying this prayer in the back of your mind all the time, it soaks into you, like dye into cotton, and colors the way you encounter every person and circumstance you meet." (brewster, ma: paraclete press, 2014), page 14.

Mother Maria Skobtsova: Essential Writings
by Mother Maria

> " He may give these hearts of ours as food for the world, that He may bring the whole world into communion with these hearts of ours that have been offered up, so that in this way we may be one with Him." (maryknoll, ny: orbis books, 2003), page 185.

Our Thoughts Determine our Lives:
the Life and Teachings of Elder Thaddeus of Vitovnica
translated by Ana Smiljanic,
compiled by St. Herman of Alaska Brotherhood

> " It is of great significance if there is a person who truly prays in a family. Prayer attracts God's Grace and all the members of the family feel it even those whose hearts have grown cold. Pray always." (platina, ca: st. herman press, 2009), page 81.

On Prayer: From the Writings of Bishop Theophan the Recluse
translated from the russian by Fr. Stefan Pavlenko, and reprinted from
Orthodox Life 32 (1982): 4.

> " Strive to experience the sweetness of pure prayer. Once experienced
> pure prayer will draw you on and enliven your spiritual life, beckoning
> you to more attentive, more difficult, and ever-deepening prayer."
> (liberty, tn: st. john of kronstadt press, 2001), page 10.

Remember Thy First Love (Revelation 2:4-5):
The Three Stages of the Spiritual Life in the Theology of Elder Sophrony
by Archimandrite Zacharias

> " If, however, we succeed in finding our deep heart, then our mind will
> drop anchor not only in the heart, but also in the depths of heaven
> where our life is 'hid with Christ in God.' And God will come and make
> His abode in us."
> (waymart, pa: mount thabor publishing, 2010), page 69.

glossary

chrism: holy oil used for anointing

compunction: blessed mourning over one's sinfulness before God

contemplation: dwelling in the presence of God

doxology: short hymn or prayer of praise

ex nihilo: out of nothing

hesychia: attentiveness to God through inner stillness

metania: make sign of the cross, reach hand toward the ground

nous: mind, spiritual control center of the soul

prostration: full bow to the ground

sacramental: visible sign of invisible grace

theosis: union with God through grace

theotokos: virgin mary, the God-bearer, mother of Jesus

troparia: byzantine hymns

yoga: a hindu physical and spiritual discipline

about the author

jennifer anna rich makes her home on a small farm near portland, oregon, with her husband, two daughters, horses, sheep, chickens, cats, and a dog. they have grown oblation papers and press since 1989, designing handmade paper goods for the portland, new york, tokyo, and paris markets.

making prayer books and prayer cards from her letterpress studio, she tends the garden, makes parchment from her saint croix sheep skins, and thanks God for the nourishing lamb chops.

with a master's degree in christianity and the arts from evangelical regent college, she loves the beauty and the holiness of the orthodox christian church, and making small steps to grow in her life of prayer.

acknowledgments

for many years i have desired *to desire* to pray, and to yearn for stillness with God each busy day. after fifty years i am still just a beginner. please forgive my presumption to offer instruction on the life of prayer. apart from the metaphoric veil of "spa" and honoring our God-given bodies with movement alongside prayer, I do not seek to say anything original. but this enduring love of the beauty of prayer in my own life moves me to speak boldly, to bring the hidden wisdom of early christian luminaries to those in the twenty-first century who may not yet have come to experience this tangible way to love your God, your neighbor, and yourself within the fabric of daily life.

of course, i could not have attempted this task without the outpouring of the many instructors and spiritual guides who have given their life's work to fortify the body of Christ in my circles. i am merely gathering the matter before me and offering it back in my quiet way. please forgive my lower-case letters. . . . they feel to me like a whisper rather than a shout.

many slim volumes exist that teach an unbroken tradition of orthodox prayer, each with individual glimmers pointing to the same deep truths. these wise teachers' words are found at the chapter headings and in supplement 3: sources for growth. seek them out, to find rich sources for further nourishment. while *prayer spa* may be a poetic introduction to the orthodox way of prayer, i urge the reader to go deeper . . . to place yourself into the gentle care of the early church, the hospital of the soul.

i am grateful to my priest of eighteen years, father theodore dorrance, who pours his life into the building up of those around him seeking truth, and who lent his time and wisdom to oversee the making of *prayer spa*.

i am inspired by and indebted to frederica mathewes-green, who gave wings to this work in many ways. and to celeste snowber, whose teachings on embodied prayer have remained buoyant in my life over these past three decades. i want to thank the generosity of those from paraclete press who believed in this book, and have guided me through the process of getting it out into the world . . . jon sweeney, michelle rich, laura mckendree, and rachel mckendree.

precious support has also come from nancy hartness, thomaida hudanish, andrea iñiguez, susan warner smith, helen stinman, and my beloved daughters, pascale and petra. but *prayer spa* would never have been written were it not for my truth-targeting husband, who believed this was a fitting task for me, and lifted me in love every step of the way.

about Paraclete Press

Who We Are

As the publishing arm of the Community of Jesus, Paraclete Press presents a full expression of Christian belief and practice–from Catholic to Evangelical, from Protestant to Orthodox, reflecting the ecumenical charism of the Community and its dedication to sacred music, the fine arts, and the written word. We publish books, recordings, sheet music, and video/DVDs that nourish the vibrant life of the church and its people.

What We Are Doing

BOOKS | The PARACLETE RECORDINGS show the richness and depth of what it means to be Christian. While Benedictine spirituality is at the heart of who we are and all that we do, our books reflect the Christian experience across many cultures, time periods, and houses of worship.

We have many series, including *Paraclete Essentials*; *Paraclete Fiction*; *Paraclete Poetry*; *Paraclete Giants*; and for children and adults, *All God's Creatures*, books about animals and faith; and *San Damiano Books*, focusing on Franciscan spirituality. Others include *Voices from the Monastery* (men and women monastics writing about living a spiritual life today), *Active Prayer*, and new for young readers: *The Pope's Cat*. We also specialize in gift books for children on the occasions of Baptism and First Communion, as well as other important times in a child's life, and books that bring creativity and liveliness to any adult spiritual life.

The MOUNT TABOR BOOKS series focuses on the arts and literature as well as liturgical worship and spirituality; it was created in conjunction with the Mount Tabor Ecumenical Centre for Art and Spirituality in Barga, Italy.

MUSIC | The PARACLETE RECORDINGS label represents the internationally acclaimed choir *Gloriæ Dei Cantores*, the *Gloriæ Dei Cantores Schola*, and the other instrumental artists of the *Arts Empowering Life Foundation*.

Paraclete Press is the exclusive North American distributor for the Gregorian chant recordings from St. Peter's Abbey in Solesmes, France. Paraclete also carries all of the Solesmes chant publications for Mass and the Divine Office, as well as their academic research publications.

In addition, PARACLETE PRESS SHEET MUSIC publishes the work of today's finest composers of sacred choral music, annually reviewing over 1,000 works and releasing between 40 and 60 works for both choir and organ.

VIDEO | Our video/DVDs offer spiritual help, healing, and biblical guidance for a broad range of life issues including grief and loss, marriage, forgiveness, facing death, understanding suicide, bullying, addictions, Alzheimer's, and Christian formation.

Learn more about us at our website:
www.paracletepress.com
or phone us toll-free at 1.800.451.5006

SCAN
TO
READ
MORE

You may also be interested in…

Putting Joy into Practice
Seven Ways to Lift Your Spirit from the Early Church
Phoebe Farag Mikhail

ISBN 978-1-64060-168-0 | $16.99 | Trade paper

Praying with the Body
Bringing the Psalms to Life
Roy DeLeon

ISBN 978-1-55725-589-1 | $19.99 | Trade paper

The Illumined Heart
Capture the Vibrant Faith of Ancient Christians
Frederica Mathewes-Green

ISBN 978-1-55725-553-2 | $18.99 | Trade paper

Available at bookstores
Paraclete Press | 1-800-451-5006
www.paracletepress.com

glory to God
for all things